Kid Pick!

Title: ______________________________

Author: ______________________________

Picked by: ______________________________

____

Why I love this book:

____

A Day in the Life: Rain Forest Animals

Piranha

Anita Ganeri

Heinemann Library
Chicago, IL

Edited by Nancy Dickmann, Rebecca Rissman, and Catherine Veitch
Designed by Steve Mead
Picture research by Mica Brancic
Originated by Capstone Global Library
Printed in the United States of America in North Mankato, Minnesota. 082013 007694RP

14 13
10 9 8 7 6 5 4 3 2

Library of Congress Cataloging-in-Publication Data
Ganeri, Anita, 1961-
Piranha / Anita Ganeri.
p. cm.—(A day in the life: rain forest animals)
Includes bibliographical references and index.
ISBN 978-1-4329-4108-6 (hc)—ISBN 978-1-4329-4119-2 (pb) 1. Piranhas—Juvenile literature. I. Title.
QL638.C5G36 2011
597'.48—dc22 2010000969

Acknowledgments
We would like to thank the following for permission to reproduce photographs: Corbis p. 5 (Science Faction/ © Norbert Wu); FLPA pp. 9 (Minden Pictures/Ingo Arndt), 16 (Gerard Lacz), 19, 22 (Minden/SA TEAM/FN), 21 (Minden Pictures/Konrad Wothe); Photolibrary pp. 4, 23 scales (Animals Animals/Jack Wilburn), 6, 13, 23 fin (Oxford Scientific (OSF)/Rodger Jackman), 7, 23 jaws (age fotostock/Darius Koehli), 10, 14, 18 (age fotostock/ Morales Morales), 11 (Oxford Scientific (OSF)/Paulo de Oliveira), 12, 23 prey (Animals Animals/Phyllis Greenberg), 15, 23 gill (Animals Animals/Zigmund Leszczynski), 17 (Oxford Scientific (OSF)/Berndt Fischer), 20 (Oxford Scientific (OSF)/Jan Aldenhoven); Shutterstock pp. 23 oxygen (© George Toubalis), 23 rain forest (© Szefei).

Cover photograph of a red-bellied piranha reproduced with permission of Getty Images (De Agostini Picture Library/C. Bevilacqua/DEA).

Back cover photographs of (left) a piranha fin reproduced with permission of Photolibrary (Animals Animals/Jack Wilburn); and (right) piranha teeth reproduced with permission of Photolibrary (age fotostock/Darius Koehli).
We would like to thank Michael Bright for his invaluable help in the preparation of this book.

Contents

Some words are in bold, **like this**. You can find them in the glossary on page 23.

What Are Piranhas?

Piranhas are a type of fish.

Piranhas have **fins** and their bodies are covered in **scales**.

There are different kinds of piranhas.

Most piranhas grow to about the size of your hand.

What Do Piranhas Look Like?

Piranhas have round bodies, big heads, and large **jaws**.

Piranhas can be blue, red, yellow, gray, or black.

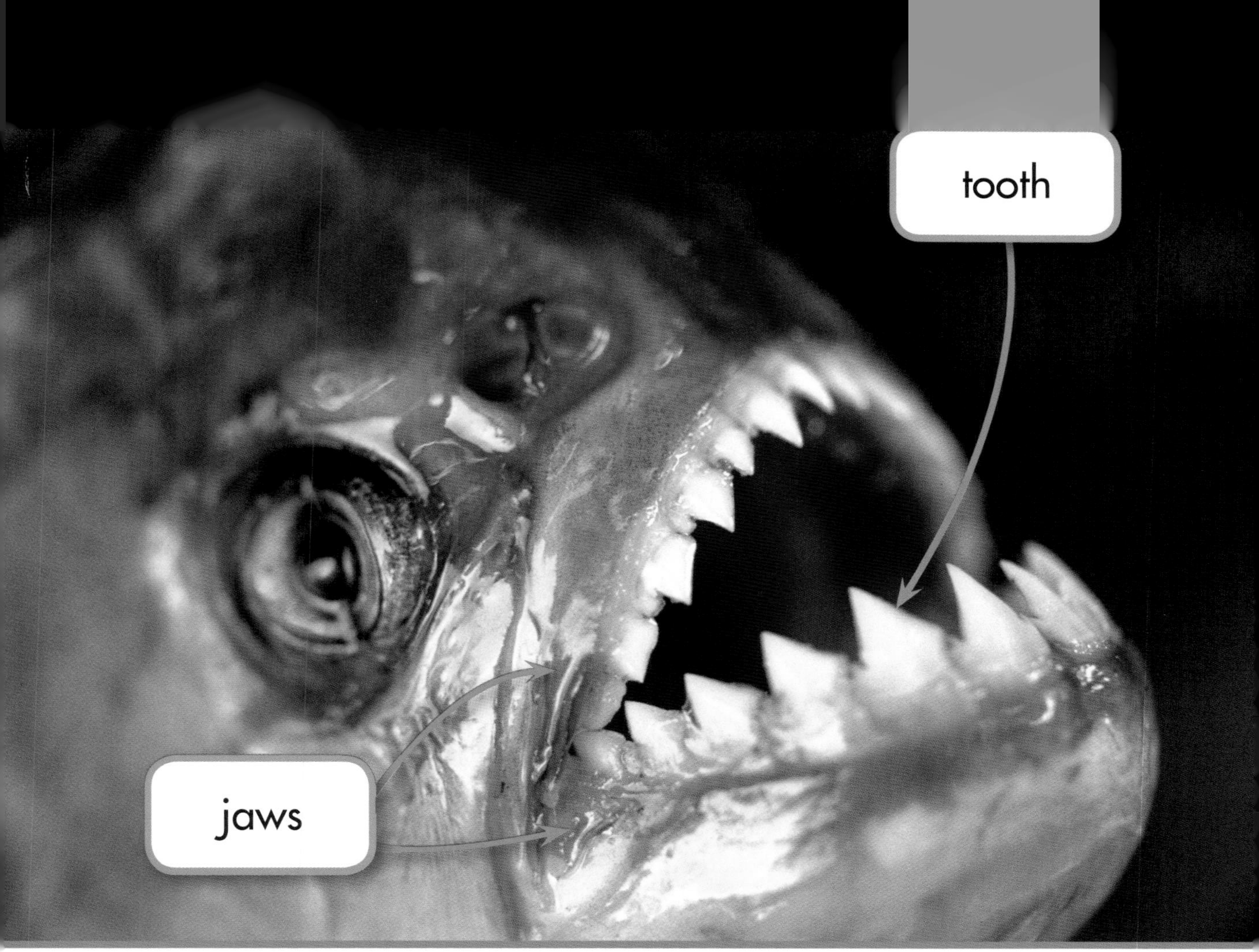

A piranha's jaws are lined with sharp, pointed teeth.

If one tooth breaks off, another tooth grows in its place.

Where Do Piranhas Live?

Piranhas live in **rain forests** in South America.

It is warm and wet in a rain forest all year long.

Piranhas live in warm water in rivers and streams.

If the water is too cold, the piranhas will die.

What Do Piranhas Do During the Day?

In the morning, piranhas start to look for food.

They swim up and down the river and hunt all day long.

Piranhas have a very good sense of smell.

They use smell to find their **prey**.

What Do Piranhas Eat?

Piranhas eat small fish, shrimps, and insects.

Some piranhas catch birds and lizards or eat dead animals.

Some piranhas eat seeds and fruit that fall into the water from trees.

A few kinds of piranhas eat the **fins** and **scales** of other fish.

How Do Piranhas Breathe?

Piranhas need **oxygen** to breathe.

They get the oxygen they need from the water around them.

Piranhas have openings in their bodies known as **gills**.

They take oxygen from water when the water moves through their gills.

Do Piranhas Live in Groups?

Piranhas live in large groups known as schools.

The piranhas stay in their schools as they swim, hunt, and rest.

Living in a school helps to keep the piranhas safe.

Animals such as caimans, find it hard to catch one fish when it is in a group.

Do People Hunt Piranhas?

During the day, people may go fishing for piranhas.

Then they cook them and eat them.

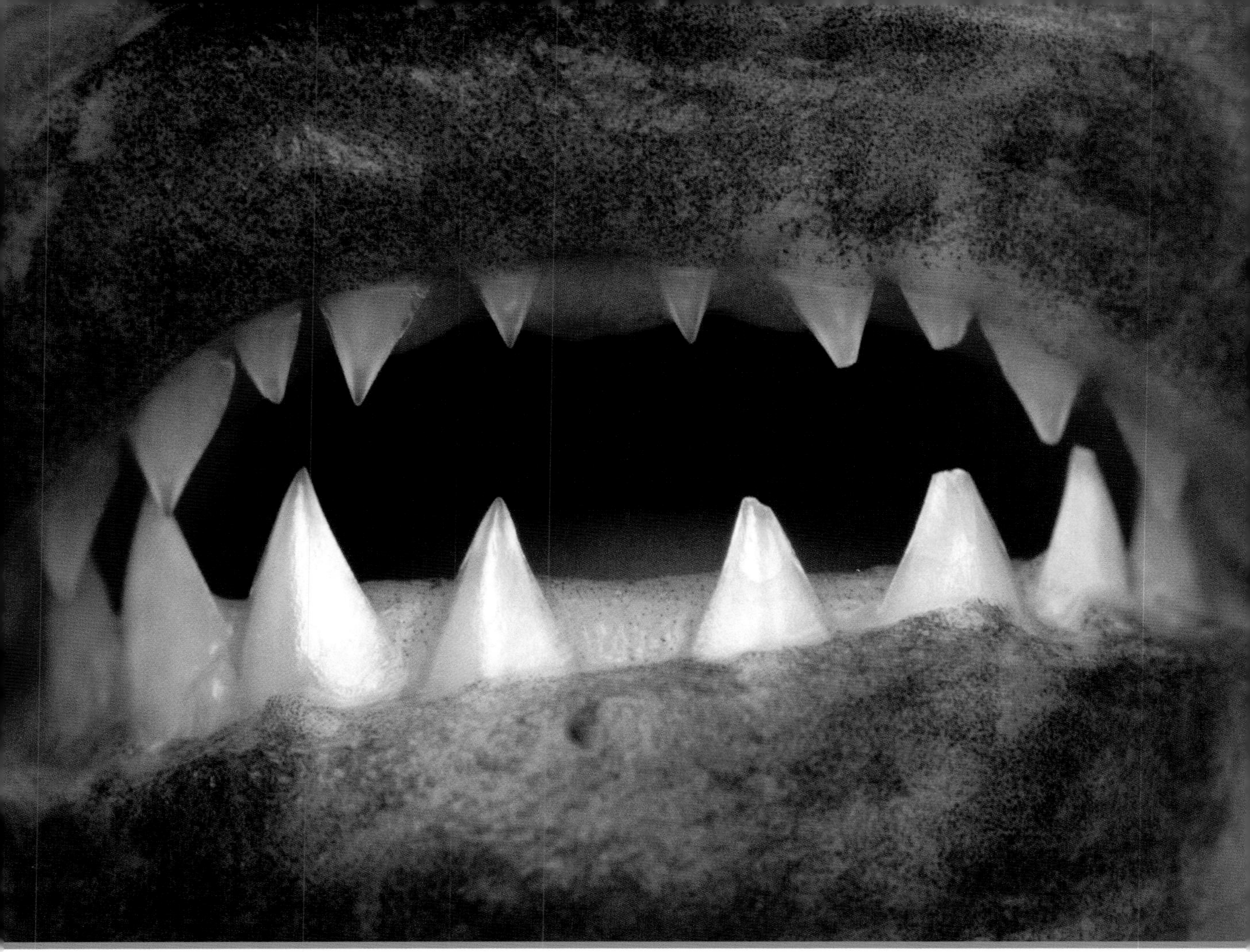

People also use piranha teeth for making tools and weapons.

A pair of scissors made from piranha teeth is very sharp.

What Do Piranhas Do at Night?

Piranhas do not go to sleep at night in the same way that you do.

Instead, they save energy by resting in the water.

Piranhas stay in their schools at night in case there is danger.

Some schools rest close to the bottom of the river. Others rest under plants.

Piranha Body Map

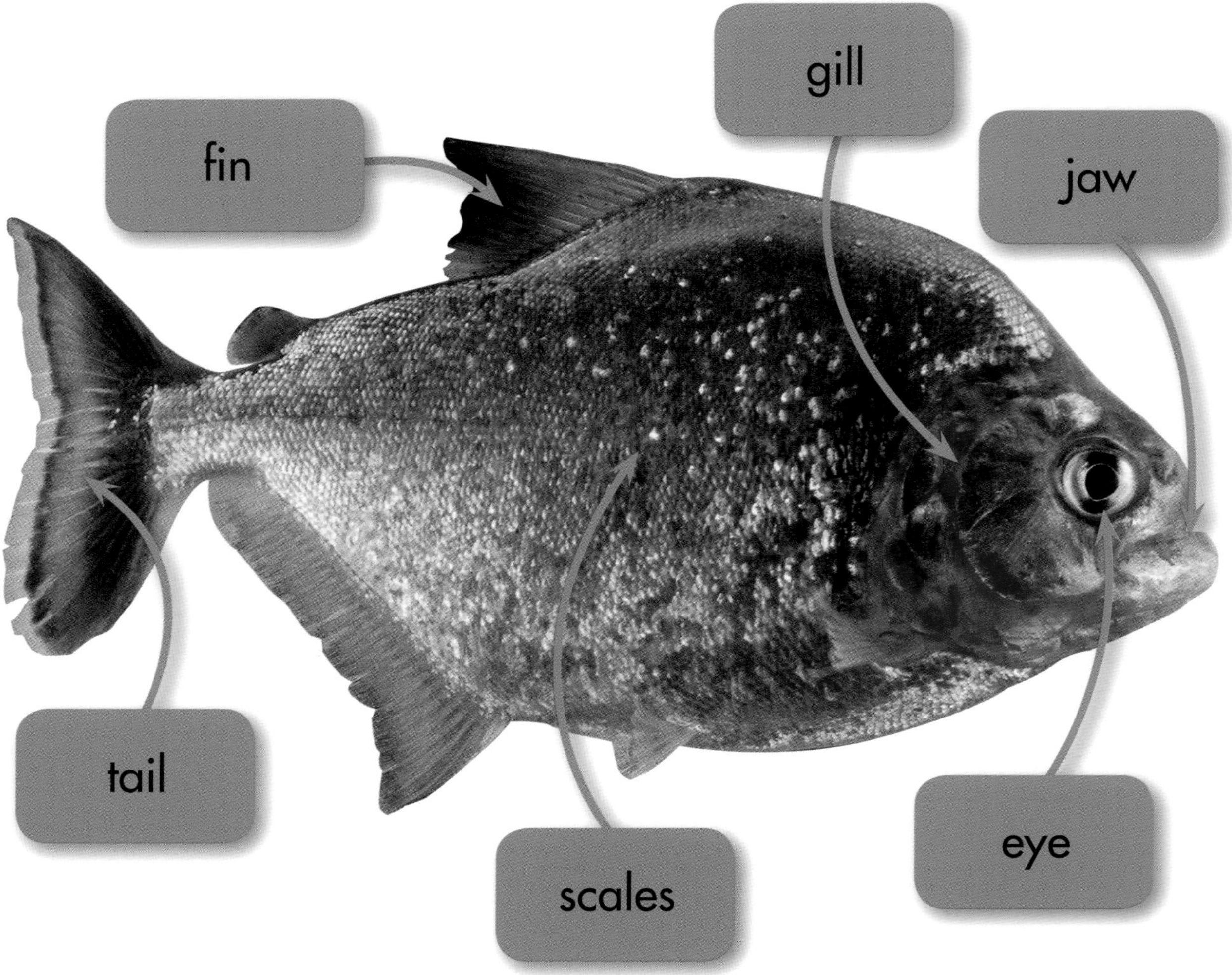

Glossary

fin flap of skin that grows from a fish's sides, back, or tail

gill part of a sea animal's body that takes air from water so the animal can breathe

jaws top and bottom parts of the mouth

oxygen gas in air and water. Animals need to breathe oxygen to stay alive.

prey animal that is hunted by other animals for food

rain forest thick forest with very tall trees and a lot of rain

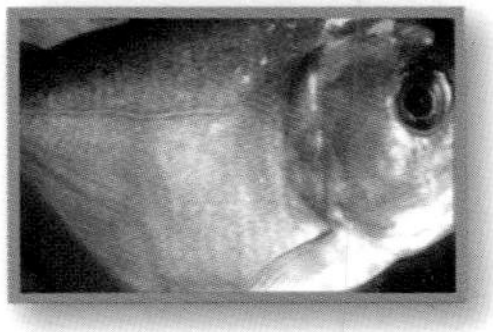

scales tiny, overlapping flaps of skin on a fish's body

Find Out More

Books

Berendes, Mary. *Piranhas.* Mankato, MN: Child's World, 2010.

Jackson, Tom. *Piranhas and Other Small Deadly Creatures.* New York, NY: Crabtree, 2009.

Websites

http://animal.discovery.com/fish/piranha/

http://a-z-animals.com/animals/piranha/

Index